THE STANDARD RESPONSE PROTOCOL
K12-T

K-12 Training Workbook
The "I Love U Guys" Foundation
SRP 2025 K12 Version 4.2 National

INSTRUCTOR GUIDE

HOLD

SECURE

LOCKDOWN

EVACUATE

SHELTER

2025 THE STANDARD RESPONSE PROTOCOL - K12-T

i love u guys
FOUNDATION

PEACE

It does not mean to be in a place where
there is no noise, trouble, or hard work.
It means to be in the midst of those things
and still be calm in your heart.

AUTHOR/CONTRIBUTOR	VERSION	REVISION DATE	REVISION COMMENTARY
John-Michael Keyes	1.0	2009-03-02	Introducing the Standard Response Protocol
John-Michael Keyes	2.0	2015-02-05	Version update. See: The Standard Response Protocol - V2 An Overview of What's New in the Standard Response Protocol
I "Love U Guys" Foundation Staff Ellen Stoddard-Keyes John-Michael Keyes	4.0	2021-04-20	Introduced Hold as an additional action. Changed the "Term of Art" Lockout to Secure. Presentation Update Instructor Guide Update
John-Michael Keyes	4.01	2021-05-10	Re-synced slide numbers. Typographical corrections.
I "Love U Guys" Foundation	4.2	2025-01-24	Expanded Cell Phone Guidance

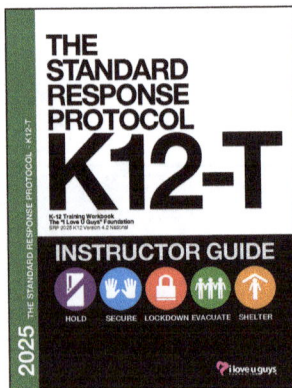

The Standard Response Protocol K12-T
Instructor Guide

Extended Versioning System:
SRP-K12.T_US_2025-v4.2.0_National-EN_S-Instructor Guide.pages
SRP-K12.T_US_2025-v4.2.0_National-EN_Instructor Guide.pdf

ISBN-13: 978-1-951260-26-2

i love u guys
FOUNDATION

FORWARD

The original concept of this program came from recognizing that most school safety plans focused on response to individual incidents. Since there is no way to predict every single type of incident, that method leaves gaps in response. It is fairly common, after a tragedy, to hear someone say "I didn't think that would happen here," so the assumption is that there was no response plan for it. Many safety plans the Foundation looked at contained similar actions being used for the various incidents, but they were called different things. The Standard Response Protocol was developed with input from many safety practitioners and is action-based, defining each physical response. When the actions are practiced and understood, they can be used almost universally for any incident. This is a life skill that stretches far beyond school. This book contains guidance on using the actions, as well as discussions and other considerations when using the Standard Response Protocol.

DEDICATION

On September 27th, 2006, a gunman entered Platte Canyon High School in Bailey, Colorado, held seven girls hostage, and ultimately shot and killed Emily Keyes. During the time she was held hostage, Emily sent her parents text messages... "I love you guys" and "I love u guys. k?" Emily's kindness, spirit, fierce joy, and the dignity and grace that followed this tragic event define the core of The "I Love U Guys" Foundation. This book is dedicated to Emily.

ACKNOWLEDGMENTS

The Keyes family is primarily grateful to responders Deputy Chief A.J. DeAndrea and Deputy Mike Denuzzi for opening the door for discussion and communication in the aftermath of the tragedy, and to former investigative reporter Paula Woodward for making the introduction. (There's a story there...) Thanks to Ted Zocco-Hochhalter for introducing us to emergency management for safer schools, to Katherine Zocco-Hochhalter for bringing humanity to the conversation, and to both for sharing their knowledge and friendship.

STAFF

The Foundation employees bring unique skills, curiosity, and intelligence to these materials, so it's all hands on deck.

BOARD OF DIRECTORS

Sometimes, nonprofits have a variety of relationships with their Boards. We have always treasured ours for their dedication and wisdom. The Foundation strives for diversity and relevant professional skills in its board of directors.

AUTHORS AND CONTRIBUTORS

The Foundation is grateful to the people who have helped with the development of the programs. For contributions to content, we are grateful to the following people:

Dr. David Benke (former teacher and former Board member) for Teacher Guidance;

Kevin Burd (Detective Lieutenant Ret., Priority of Life Training and Consulting) for content contribution and training expertise;

Russell Deffner (Advisor/Contractor/Volunteer) for Incident Command Guidance;

Pat Hamilton (Chief Operating Officer, Adams 12 Five Star School District Ret.) for years of content contributions;

Tom Kelley (Director of Readiness, Texas Education Agency) for content contributions;

Ian Lopez (Director of Safety & Security, Cherry Creek Schools) for content contributions;

John McDonald (Executive Director, Safety, Security and Emergency Planning, Jefferson County Public Schools, Ret.) for ongoing discussion and input on what's really going on in the world;

Joleen Reefe (City and County of Broomfield Ret.) for the phrase, "Locks, Lights, Out of Sight";

Jaclyn Schildkraut PhD (Executive Director, Regional Gun Violence Research Consortium, Rockefeller Institute of Government) for accuracy and research on drills and drill guidance;

Heidi Walts (Commander, Firestone Police Department) for being the best sister and sister-in-law to John-Michael and Ellen, and also giving excellent guidance when they needed it the most.

CONTACT INFORMATION

The "I Love U Guys" Foundation can be reached online at https://iloveuguys.org.

Email: srp@iloveuguys.org

Mail to: The "I Love U Guys" Foundation
PO Box 489, Placitas, NM 87043
Answering service: 303.426.3100

"Tactics are intel driven."

What we plan is based on what we know.

"But the environment dictates tactics."

What we do is based on where we are.

*– **Deputy Chief A.J. DeAndrea***
– Civilian Translation: John-Michael Keyes

LIGHT TABLE

SRP 2025 CLASSROOM TRAINING
RGB Red Green Blue
RGB Red Green Blue
SOUNDCHECK
VIDEO CHECK
i love u guys
SRP-2025
SRP-2025 Standard Response Protocol
SHARED LEXICON
SHARED WITH
SHARED WITH
SHARED WITH
SHARED WITH
EACH ACTION
EVERY ACTION
PUBLIC ADDRESS
HOLD!
WHY?
WHY?
STUDENT
STUDENTS
TEACHER
TEACHERS
TEACHERS
TEACHERS
TEACHERS
DISCUSSION:
DISCUSSION:
SECURE
WHY SECURE ?
CRIMINAL
CIVIL
DANGEROUS
GET INSIDE
INSIDE
STUDENT
STUDENTS
STUDENTS
STUDENTS
TEACHER
TEACHERS
TEACHERS
TEACHERS
TEACHERS
TEACHERS
LIFECYCLE
LIFECYCLE
LIFECYCLE
DISCUSSION:
DISCUSSION:
DISCUSSION:
DISCUSSION:
LOCKDOWN!
WHY?
WRONG
WEAPON
SOMETHING
TIME BARRIER
70% OVER IN 5
90% OVER IN 10
SANDY HOOK
SANDY HOOK
SANDY HOOK
SOLID CORE DOOR
STEEL FRAME JAMB
INDUSTRIAL STRENGTH MECHANISMS
STUDENT
LOCKDOWN!
LOCKDOWN
STUDENTS
STUDENTS
TEACHER
STUDENTS
LOCKS
LIGHTS
OUT OF SIGHT
TEACHERS
EXTERIOR SHADES
TEACHERS
TEACHERS
TEACHERS
LOCKDOWN!
LOCKDOWN!
DISCUSSION:
DISCUSSION:
DISCUSSION:
DISCUSSION:
DISCUSSION:
EVACUATE
STUDENT
STUDENTS
STUDENTS
STUDENTS
TEACHER
TEACHERS
OTHER OPTIONS
STUDENTS
STUDENTS
POLICE
POLICE
STUDENT
STUDENTS
STUDENTS
STUDENTS
STUDENTS
TEACHER
TEACHERS
TEACHERS
TEACHERS
DISCUSSION:
DISCUSSION:
DISCUSSION:
DISCUSSION:
DISCUSSION:
DISCUSSION:
SHELTER
HAZARD?
STRATEGY
TORNADO
EARTHQUAKE
HAZMAT
TSUNAMI
DURING SHELTER
DURING SHELTER
TEACHERS
SRP-2025
HANDOUTS
PEACE.
i love u guys

THE "I LOVE U GUYS" FOUNDATION

On September 27th, 2006 a gunman entered Platte Canyon High School in Bailey, Colorado, held seven girls hostage, and ultimately shot and killed Emily Keyes. During the time she was held hostage, Emily sent her parents text messages... "I love you guys" and "I love u guys. k?" Emily's kindness, spirit, fierce joy, and the dignity and grace that followed this tragic event define the core of The "I Love U Guys" Foundation.

MISSION

The "I Love U Guys" Foundation was created to restore and protect the joy of youth through educational programs and positive actions in collaboration with families, schools, communities, organizations and government entities.

COMMITMENT

There are several things we are committed to. The most important thing we can do is offer our materials at no cost to schools, districts, departments, agencies, and organizations. The reason we are able to continue to provide this service is due, in part, to the generosity of our donors and Mission Partners (see Partner with Love on the website). The "I Love U Guys" Foundation works very hard to keep our costs down as well as any costs associated with our printed materials. Donor and Mission Partner support allows us to stretch those dollars and services even more. Your gift, no matter the size, helps us achieve our mission. Your help makes a difference to the students, teachers, first responders, and the communities in which we live and work.

WARNINGS AND DISCLAIMER

Every effort has been made to make this book as complete and accurate as possible, but no warranty or fitness is implied. The information provided is on an "as is" basis. Please visit our website (https://iloveuguys.org) for detailed information. There are some links to resources in this book. In most PDFs, they will be clickable, but the Foundation cannot guarantee that the actual source is still available at that site.

COPYRIGHTS AND TRADEMARKS

In order to protect the integrity and consistency of the Standard Response Protocol, The "I Love U Guys" Foundation exercises all protection under copyright and trademark. Use of this material is governed by the Terms of Use (details in the MOU and NOI documents) or a Commercial Licensing Agreement.

COMMERCIAL LICENSING

Incorporating the SRP into a commercial product, like software or publication, requires a licensing agreement. Please contact The "I Love U Guys" Foundation for more information and costs.

ABOUT SRP 2025

The "I Love U Guys" Foundation is committed to reviewing Standard Response Protocol materials every two years.

For SRP 2023, there was expanded guidance, the introduction of the "SRP Lockdown Drill," and new communications guidance. SRP 2025 builds on 2023 and offers further guidance on the use of each action.

As you begin to implement and drill the protocol, keep in mind that environments are different. What that means is that we provide you with some tactics. Things we know. But your school, your agencies, and your environment will ultimately dictate what you do.

THE "I LOVE U GUYS" FOUNDATION MOU

Some schools, districts, departments, and agencies may desire a formalized Memorandum of Understanding (MOU) with The "I Love U Guys" Foundation. For a current version of the MOU, please visit iloveuguys.org.

The purpose of an MOU is to define the responsibilities of each party and provide scope and clarity of expectations. It affirms the agreement of stated protocol by schools, districts, departments, and agencies. It also confirms the online availability of the Foundation's materials.

An additional benefit for the Foundation is in seeking funding. Some private grantors view the MOU as a demonstration of program effectiveness. This can be emailed to srp@iloveuguys.org

NOTICE OF INTENT

Another option is to formally notify the Foundation with a Notice of Intent (NOI). This is a notice that you are reviewing the materials but have not adopted them yet. This is also available on the website.

Minimally, schools, districts, departments, and agencies that are assessing the SRP and plan to incorporate the program into their safety plans and practices should email srp@iloveuguys.org and let The Foundation know.

FAIR USE POLICY

These materials are for educational and informational purposes only and may contain copyrighted material the use of which has not always been specifically authorized by the copyright owner. In accord with our nonprofit mission, we are making such material available for the public good to restore and protect the joy of youth through educational programs and positive actions in collaboration with families, schools, communities, organizations, and government entities.

The "I Love U Guys" Foundation IRS 501(c)3 est. 2006 asserts this constitutes a 'fair use' of any such copyrighted material as provided in Section 107 of the US Copyright Law. In accordance with Title 17 U.S.C. Section 107, these materials are distributed without profit to those who have expressed a prior interest in receiving the included information for criticism, comment, news reporting, teaching, scholarship, education and research.

If you wish to use copyrighted material from this site for purposes of your own that go beyond fair use, you must obtain permission from copyright owner. If your copyrighted material appears in our materials and you disagree with our assessment that it constitutes 'fair use', contact us.

PRIVACY POLICY

When you agree to the Terms of Use by sending an MOU or NOI, your contact information will be entered into a database. You will receive notification when there are updates and/or new materials. You will have the opportunity to opt-in to receive periodic blog posts and newsletters via email.

OUR COMMITMENT TO PROGRAM USERS:

We will not sell, share, or trade names, contact, or personal information with any other entity, nor send mailings to our donors on behalf of other organizations. This policy applies to all information received by The "I Love U Guys" Foundation, both online and offline, as well as any electronic, written, or oral communications. Please see our website for the full Privacy text.

TERMS OF USE

Schools, districts, departments, agencies and organizations may use these materials, at no cost, under the following conditions:

1. Materials are not re-sold
2. Core actions and directives are not modified
   2.1. **Hold** "In your room or area."
   2.2. **Secure** "Get inside. Lock outside doors"
   2.3. **Lockdown** "Locks. Lights. Out of sight."
   2.4. **Evacuate** A Location may be specified
   2.5. **Shelter** State the hazard and the safety strategy.
3. The Notification of Intent (NOI) is used when the materials are being evaluated. A sample NOI can be downloaded from the website, and is provided to The "I Love U Guys" Foundation through one of the following:
   3.1. Complete the NOI and email it to srp@iloveuguys.org
   3.2. Send an email to srp@iloveuguys.org
4. The Memorandum of Understating (MOU) is used when it has been determined that the materials will be used. A sample MOU can be downloaded from iloveuguys.org, and is provided to The "I Love U Guys" Foundation by emailing it to srp@iloveuguys. org
5. The following modifications to the materials are allowable:
   5.1. Localization of Evacuation events
   5.2. Localization of Shelter events
   5.3. Addition of the organization logo

ONE DEMAND

The protocol also carries an obligation. Kids and teens are smart. An implicit part of the SRP is that authorities and school personnel tell students what's going on.

Certainly, temper it at the elementary school level, but middle schoolers and older need accurate information for the greatest survivability, and to minimize panic and assist recovery.

Note: Student training includes preparation for some alternative methods during a tactical response, but reinforces deference to local law enforcement.

The Standard Response Protocol is a synthesis of common practices in use at a number of districts, departments and agencies. The evolution of SRP has included review, comment and suggestion from a number of practitioners. With each version, the SRP is subjected to tactical scrutiny by law enforcement agencies and operational review and adoption by schools. Suggestions for modification can be made via email at srp_rfc@iloveuguys.org. Please include contact information, district, department, or agency, including daytime phone.

ABOUT THE PRESENTATION

The presentation has been developed to assist law enforcement, school, or district personnel in rapidly training students, teachers, and other stakeholders the common language, actions and expectations of The Standard Response Protocol (SRP).

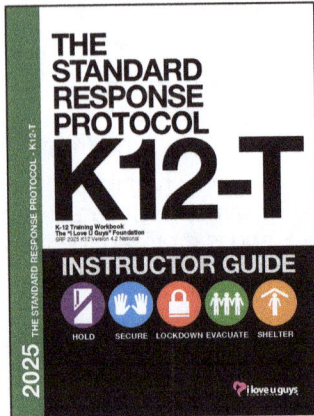

This workbook has been developed to assist presenters in learning the SRP presentation. It replaces the first version of the training presentation and the changes are based on the experience of over 100 personally delivered presentations. You can download a PDF of this workbook and the associated presentation in PowerPoint or Keynote, at no charge, by visiting http://iloveuguys.org.

ABOUT THE BOOK

The "I Love U Guys" Foundation is committed to providing digital material online, at no charge to districts, departments or agencies.

Through Amazon you can also purchase physical books. All proceeds and/or royalties from these purchases go to the The "I Love U Guys" Foundation.

We recognize the budget constraints that many districts are feeling and have attempted to keep prices reasonable. We strongly suggest that you compare costs and use the downloadable versions of all materials since those are free.

NOT YOUR TYPICAL POWERPOINT

You've probably noticed that the presentation isn't your "typical" powerpoint. No bullet lists. Lots of images. In fact, with only a couple of exceptions, slides have no more than seven words. Per slide! There are reasons for this. In fact, there is science behind it.

But the notion is simple. Too many words per slide causes cognitive overload and reduces your audience's learning capacity. By separating concepts, you give each concept time to sink in. It also means that some slides will only be shown for a few moments. You are going to get very good with a clicker.

AN AWKWARD INTRODUCTION

John-Michael Keyes did a ton of research on presentation development and multimedia learning theory when creating his presentations on the SRP and the training materials. In 2010 he wrote *"Carpe Audience – Deliver Better Presentations, Despite PowerPoint,"* documenting both the method and the madness... uh... science behind the technique.

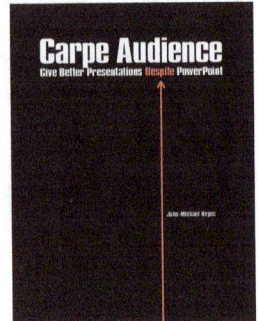

It was, and is, not his intent to use the SRP to promote his book, but an interesting thing happened. School Resource Officers became interested in the method. It makes sense. They are often in the classroom or the training room delivering presentations. Educators got interested. Even the local Chamber of Commerce.

That's our awkward introduction to a valuable resource: "Carpe Audience." You can download the PDF version, at no cost, from iloveuguys.org,

GETTING STARTED

Take a moment and page through this book. You'll see the slides presented on the outside edge with the spoken script on the inside of the page. We've deliberately left some room if you need to add your own notes.

It's not a bad idea to fire up PowerPoint (or Keynote on the Mac) at this point and familiarize yourself with the slides. If the presentation didn't open with the presenter notes visible, take a moment and show them.

The presenter notes are the same as the script in this book. An often overlooked feature with both PowerPoint and Keynote is the presenter display. By configuring your computer for multi-monitor display, the projector can display your slides and the laptop can display your presenter notes. If you haven't used the presenter notes feature in PowerPoint or Keynote, while delivering a presentation, it's worth the effort to figure out how to enable the feature.

THE SETUP SLIDES

The first few slides are designed to help you achieve the best audio and visual support for your presentation. These are for setup only and should be advanced prior to the audience being in the room. These slides also provide another purpose. With larger venues, there is often an AV technician or IT person assigned to assist in setup. These slides demonstrate that this is an important presentation and you are concerned about the audience getting the best experience.

CUSTOMIZE

There is an option to customize the slides. Localizing some of the images or introducing some site specific challenges or opportunities can increase effectiveness. Look for the "Do-it-yourself" icon on the slides that should be localized. That said, please respect the Terms of Use (Page 5). Please don't use these or other Foundation SRP materials if you change the five actions and directives.

There is another aspect of customization. If you are adding your own content, use the Master Slides so the formatting matches. And please, resist the bullet list. Really. Presentations are far more effective when there are fewer words on screen. Instead, separate your concepts and find some images that support them. It's ok if any individual slide isn't projected for a great period of time.

TRUST BUT VERIFY

Several of the slides should be verified with local authorities, district-wide school safety team and/or building-level emergency response team(s), as appropriate. The SRP offers instructions for each action and directive. It also suggests current guidance regarding some generic hazards and safety strategies. Look for the "Trust but verify" icon on a slide. Your training for students and staff should include any specific details that are unique to your district or school.

VIDEO CLIPS

When video clips are used, look for the "Play" icon. We've included the transcript of the video as well. As you start working with the slides, you'll notice that prior to any video playing, the "Play" triangle cues you that the next slide will autostart a video.

OPTIONAL

Some sections of the presentation are optional. The slides that are optional are indicated with the "Optional" icon on the slide.

When presenting to younger audiences feel free to hide any slide that isn't age appropriate.

MECHANICALS

This version of the presentation was initially developed in Keynote 5.4 (iWork '09) in January of 2015. The resolution is set to 1280 px. x 720 px. The font used is Helvetica Neue Bold sized at either 144 pt. or 64 pt. This font ships with recent Macintosh computers or is installed by recent OS X updates.

The Windows version of this presentation has been exported to PowerPoint and any conversion issues resolved. The font was embedded in its entirety as a PowerPoint option during file creation.

The video resources have been encoded for native display on both Windows and Mac.

DON'T FORGET TO REHEARSE

If you haven't delivered this presentation before, take 20 or 30 minutes to rehearse it. Not just sit there and read it, but stand up and say it out loud. Launch PowerPoint or Keynote on your computer, and go through the presentation as if your screen was your audience.

**SRP 2025
CLASSROOM TRAINING
AV SETUP**

Extended Versioning System:
SRP K12.T_NY_2025-v4.2_NYSED-EN_Classroom Training.key
SRP K12.T_NY_2025-v4.2_NYSED-EN_Classroom Training.pptx

i love u guys

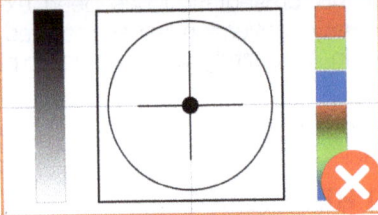

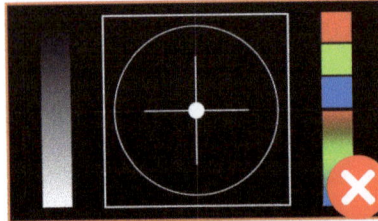

	This is a projector calibration slide. The squares in the upper right should be red, green, blue from top down. If any of these are black, then the projector lamp is faulty. The center circle and square should not be an oval or rectangle. If they are, then you may need to change the resolution for the projector on your laptop.
RGB Red Green Blue	This is a second RGB verification. If any of the colors are black, then replace the lamp or projector.
	This is a projector calibration slide. The squares in the upper right should be red, green, blue from top down. If any of these are black, then the projector lamp is faulty. The center circle and square should not be an oval or rectangle. If they are, then you may need to change the resolution for the projector on your laptop.
RGB Red Green Blue	This is a second RGB verification. If any of the colors are black, then replace the lamp or projector.
	Image test **DIY: Replace this with a photo of your own.**
SOUNDCHECK ▶	Sound check
VIDEO CHECK ▶	This is a neat snippet from the Aspen PD and Pitkin County Sheriff's Office in Colorado. If you are training little ones, view this first.

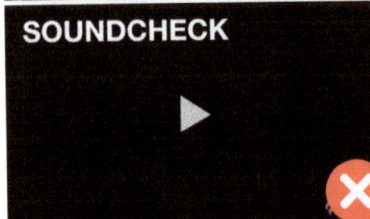

We are going to spend a few minutes talking about the Standard Response Protocol.	
You have probably seen this poster around the school and noticed the icons.	
We are going to talk about what these five icons mean. Schools are adopting a standard to enhance student and staff safety during an incident or emergency.	
The key to the Standard Response Protocol is that there is a simple, shared lexicon between staff, parents, students, and first responders. And when used, everyone involved shares the same expectations. What is a lexicon? It is a vocabulary. Who are we sharing it with?	
We start with first responders. So if something happens at our school, they'll know what to do.	
Teachers and staff are given the same training.	
The same language is shared with students. So you know what to do.	

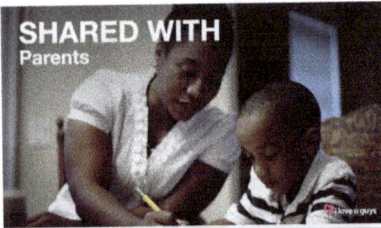

SHARED WITH Parents	And it's also important to tell your parents what you will learn today.
STANDARD RESPONSE PROTOCOL	Remember, it is called the Standard Response Protocol.
HOLD SECURE LOCKDOWN EVACUATE SHELTER	It is based on five actions that we take during an incident or an emergency. Hold, Secure, Lockdown, Evacuate, and Shelter.
EACH ACTION Is Always Followed by a Directive — HOLD SECURE LOCKDOWN EVACUATE SHELTER	Each action is followed by a directive.
EVERY ACTION Has specific instructions — HOLD SECURE LOCKDOWN EVACUATE SHELTER	Every action then has specific instructions of what to do in an emergency.
PUBLIC ADDRESS Action and Directive is Repeated	When these are called on the PA, the action and directive are repeated.
HOLD! In your classroom	Hold in your classroom. Hold in your classroom.
WHY? The halls need to be kept clear.	It's used when we need to keep the corridors clear of students. It might be a medical emergency or a hazmat spill in the hallways.

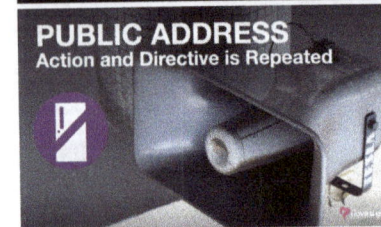

Or something else that needs a cleanup. A hold may be localized to one area of the school, or it could be for the entire school.	**WHY?** The halls need to be kept clear.
Here's what students do.	**STUDENT** Instructions
If you're in the hallway, go to your assigned classroom. Otherwise, students and teachers remain in their classrooms until the "All Clear" is announced.	**STUDENTS** Remain in the classroom until all clear.
Teachers, here's what you do.	**TEACHER** Instructions
Remain in the classroom with your students until the "All Clear" is announced.	**TEACHERS** Remain in the classroom until all clear.
Teachers should also close and lock the door. It can be opened for any student that needs to get out of the corridor.	**TEACHERS** Close and lock the classroom door.
Teachers should also verify that everyone is still in class. It's a good idea to note the time that attendance was taken.	**TEACHERS** Take attendance and note the time
Continue teaching. Or if the lesson for the day is complete, offer time to read or study.	**TEACHERS** Business as usual.

DISCUSSION: What about class changes?	What about class changes? You will remain in your class even if the bell rings. If you're in the hallway, public address might be made to go to the nearest classroom. Or, proceed to your next scheduled class.
DISCUSSION: Is this a Lockdown?	Is this a Lockdown? No, we'll talk more about Lockdown in a bit. With the Hold protocol, we just don't want what's happening in the hallway to spill into the classroom. Students remain in their seats, continue lessons, or if lessons are done, students may be given time to read or study. No drama here.
SECURE Get Inside. Lock Outside Doors	Secure! Get inside. Lock outside doors. Secure! Get inside. Lock outside doors.
WHY SECURE ? Something dangerous near the school	Why? There is a threat outside of the building.
CRIMINAL Activity in the area	Might be criminal activity.
CIVIL Unrest	Or civil unrest.
DANGEROUS Animal on the playground	Or a dangerous animal outside.
GET INSIDE Lock outside doors	If there are exterior doors in the classroom, make sure they're locked. Teachers may also be asked to check if nearby exterior doors are locked.

Almost always, it's business as usual in the building.	**INSIDE** Business as usual
Let's start with student instructions on what to do in a Secure protocol.	**STUDENT** Instructions
First one is simple. Get in the building. For the most part, it is business as usual inside the building.	**STUDENTS** Get in the building
If Secure lasts into recess or lunch, no one in or out. So we're staying in the building. Same thing is true at the end of the school day. Depending on what's going on we may have to stay in the building, or students that walk home may have to call their parents to be picked up.	**STUDENTS** Then, no one in or out
Business as usual inside the school building.	**STUDENTS** Business as usual
Let's look at what a teacher should do during Secure.	**TEACHER** Instructions
Bring everyone inside. But that brings up a question about notification when students or staff are outside. How are they notified? Radio system? PA system? Make sure the staff knows what you'll use in your school.	**TEACHERS** Bring everyone inside
If there are exterior doors in the classroom, make sure they're locked. Teachers may also be asked to check if nearby exterior doors are are locked.	**TEACHERS** Lock outside doors

TEACHERS Increase situational awareness	Increase situational awareness. You know, be attentive.
TEACHERS Take attendance and note the time	Teachers should also verify that everyone is still in class. It's a good idea to note the time that attendance was taken.
TEACHERS Business as usual	Almost always, it's business as usual in the building.
LIFECYCLE No one in or out	There is a lifecycle during Secure. Staff will lock all outside doors. And initially no one is allowed in or out.
LIFECYCLE Controlled Release	Secure can evolve into a controlled release. Depending on the incident, it can eventually be safe to release students to parents. We call that a controlled release.
LIFECYCLE Monitored Entry	Or Secure can evolve into a monitored entry. Depending on the incident, it might be safe to monitor who is allowed to enter the school building.
DISCUSSION: When might a Secure occur?	What are the reasons for Secure? When there is a threat or danger outside of the school. We talked about some, here are some more. Bank robbery, high speed chase, suspicious person, riots, demonstrations, custody issue, maybe a fire in the neighborhood.
DISCUSSION: Who can call a Secure ?	Who can call Secure? Student: by reporting to staff member Teacher: by reporting to main office More likely, the school receives the call from police and should initiate the Secure protocol within the school. This should occur without having to go through a chain of command.

What about class changes?	**DISCUSSION:** What about class changes?
Most of the time, it is business as usual. Normal, in-building class changes occur. If a threat is very close to the school, the response may be to go into Secure rather than Lockdown.	
If a school has modular buildings, students and staff may be brought into the main building.	
Can we leave the school?	**DISCUSSION:** Can we leave the school?
Usually not. There is something dangerous near the school. This means that even if the school day ends, we may have to stay in the building until the threat is mitigated.	
Lockdown is more serious.	**LOCKDOWN** Locks, Lights, Out of Sight!
Lockdown. Locks, lights, out of sight.	
Lockdown. Locks, lights, out of sight.	
Lockdown is used when there is a threat inside the school building.	**WHY?** Something dangerous inside the building
Could be the wrong person.	**WRONG** Person
Maybe a weapon report.	**WEAPON** Report
Or something worse. An armed intruder or some other threat inside the building.	**SOMETHING** Worse
We want to introduce the notion of time barriers. And it turns out that a locked classroom door is a proven time barrier.	**TIME BARRIER**

70% OVER IN 5 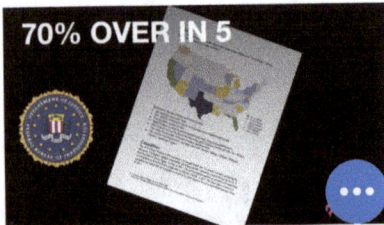	The US Department of Justice has studied these events. 70% are over in 5 minutes.
90% OVER IN 10 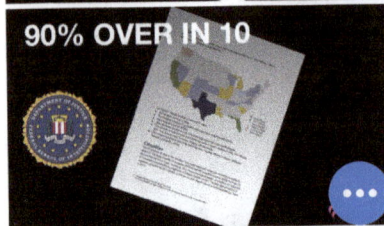	90% are over in 10.
SANDY HOOK Commission 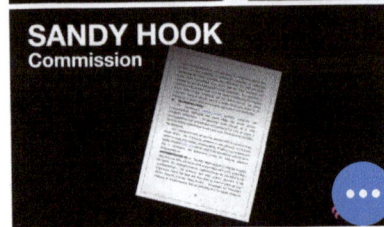	In 2015, the Sandy Hook Commission released their summary report. The number 1 environmental design recommendation was the ability to lock the classroom door from inside the classroom.
SANDY HOOK Commission 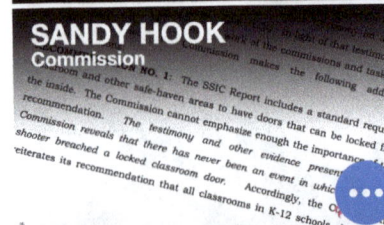	Not just teachers but subs as well. Why? Their testimony, their research found zero cases of a gunman breaching a locked classroom door. Zero.
SANDY HOOK Commission 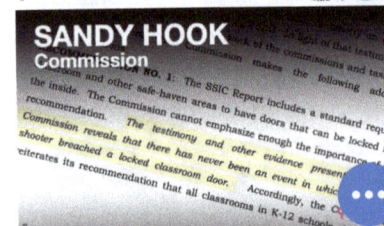	The Foundation expanded the scope and there is an edge case. Red Lake Minnesota the gunman breached the side windows by the classroom door to gain entry.
SOLID CORE DOOR 	Classroom doors for the last 30 years have had solid core doors…
STEEL FRAME JAMB 	…steel frame jambs…
INDUSTRIAL STRENGTH MECHANISMS 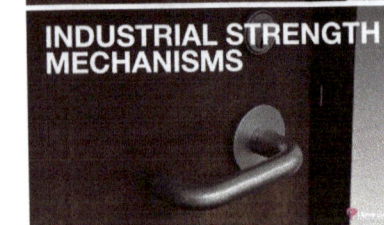	…and industrial strength locking mechanisms.

Voice Over:

If you are in a classroom when a Lockdown is called, the main thing to remember is "Locks. Lights. Out of sight."

As students gather in a safe area of the room, lock the door and turn off all lights.

Have everyone in the room move to a location that is out of sight. Pick an area of the room that can't be seen from any interior window.

An actual lockdown may not be resolved for several hours.

Here's how you should wait: Stay in the safe location. Don't move around the room. Remain silent.

Staff: Take written attendance of who is in the room. Note anyone missing or any extra students or staff.

STUDENT
Instructions

LOCKDOWN!
Locks, Lights, Out of Sight.

Locks. Lights. Out of sight.

LOCKDOWN!
Locks, Lights, Out of Sight.

First stay out of sight from the corridor window. How do you know you're out of sight? If you can't see out the corridor window, no one in the hall can see you. Also sit on the floor and get low.

A locked door is proven time barrier. In active violence events, rarely, if ever, has someone been hurt who was behind a locked classroom door.

STUDENTS
Stay out of sight of the corridor window

Be absolutely silent. Turn your phone off in the initial stages of a Lockdown. (If there is an actual Lockdown, you may get a chance to text your parents in a while.)

STUDENTS
Be silent

Do not open the door for anyone. Law Enforcement will unlock the door and release the room.

In the case of a room having students or staff with special needs or abilities, an Administrator may offer a familiar face and will accompany Law Enforcement.

STUDENTS
Do not open the door for anyone

Let's look at what teachers should do in a Lockdown.

TEACHER
Instructions

When you hear "Lockdown! Locks, lights out of sight," sweep the hallway for students. If the threat is close to your classroom, focus on getting the door locked and closed as quickly as possible. A locked classroom door is a proven lifesaver.

LOCKS
Lock and close the classroom door

LIGHTS Turn out the lights	Turn out the lights.
OUT OF SIGHT If you can't see the corridor window... It can't see you.	Be silent and maintain student silence. Turn off your phone.
TEACHERS Covered or uncovered	Leave the corridor window as it is. In general, you should leave these door window panels uncovered so that in an emergency, first responders can see into the room from the hallway. Law enforcement needs to see into the room from the hallway. Science rooms often have two doors with corridor windows, making it difficult to get out of sight. In this case, it may be beneficial to cover one of the corridor windows. ✓ **Verify this direction with local law enforcement.**
TEACHERS	More law enforcement agencies are recommending ***not*** sliding red/green cards under the door. The reasoning is two-fold. First, they won't believe the message until they have verified the status of the classroom. And, you are giving too much information to the bad guy. ✓ **Verify this direction with local law enforcement.**
EXTERIOR SHADES Leave alone	If it is open leave it open, if it is closed leave it closed. You would probably be in sight of the corridor window when you are adjusting the shades.
TEACHERS Maintain silence	Turn off your phone. If you are with young students, it may be soothing to very quietly read to them. A Lockdown cannot be ended with a PA announcement. It only ends with police opening the door and releasing the room.
TEACHERS Take attendance and note the time	If you can, take attendance. Note if you have missing students, or extra students swept from the hall. Note the time. You probably won't need to do anything with the roster at this point, but we're creating a chain of custody and this will be useful over the lifecycle of the event.
LOCKDOWN! Locks, Lights, Out of Sight.	Let's look at this.

Voice Over:
If a fire alarm sounds, do not leave your safe location unless you are certain a fire is threatening your room.

If you are forced to evacuate due to a fire, keep in mind that the hall may not be your best escape route.

Verify this direction with local fire department. ✓

LOCKDOWN!
Locks, Lights, Out of Sight.

What if you're outside?

If you're outside and a Lockdown is called, do not go back into the building. Rather, go to a safe location. Make sure you notify the school of your location.

DISCUSSION:
What if you're outside?

What if there is no teacher?

Getting behind a locked door if possible. If not, close the door and get out of sight.

Or you may try to evacuate if the threat is not in your immediate vicinity.

DISCUSSION:
What if there's no teacher?

What if you're in the hallway?

Teachers check the halls quickly before they lock the door and turn the lights out. Get to a classroom, any classroom, as quickly as you can and lockdown.

If the classroom is already locked, then find a place to hide. Do not go from classroom to classroom. Evacuating may be another option.

DISCUSSION:
What if you're in the hallway?

What if the fire alarm sounds?

Stay in the classroom unless you see fire or if smoke is filling your classroom. If you must evacuate due to a fire or smoke, the hallway may not be your best option. Consider using an alternate door, window, or any other exterior exit.

DISCUSSION:
What if the fire alarm sounds?

Can we text our parents?

Craft this messaging per local or state guidelines ✓

DISCUSSION:
Can we text our parents?

Evacuate is how to move students in an orderly fashion from point A to point B. A fire drill is really: "Evacuate Out of the Building."

With the SRP, Evacuate is always followed by a predetermined safe location. For instance:

Evacuate to the gym. Evacuate to the gym.

EVACUATE
To a location

So, here's what students do.

STUDENT
Instructions

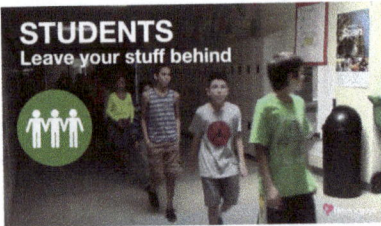

STUDENTS Leave your stuff behind	Usually, you leave your stuff behind.
STUDENTS Bring your stuff	Sometimes, you may be asked to bring your stuff.
STUDENTS Listen for directions	Be sure to listen for any new directions.
TEACHER Instructions	Teachers, there may be times when you lead the students out, but sometimes you may be asked to follow your students out. In a police led evacuation, you'll probably be asked to lead the students.
TEACHERS At evacuation area take attendance	Teachers at the evacuation area take attendance and note the time.
OTHER OPTIONS Rapidly Self Evacuate	During an active violence event, another option is to rapidly self evacuate.
STUDENTS Self Evacuation	
STUDENTS Self Evacuation	

Voice Over:

During the initial moments of a school violence situation, the official call for a lockdown may not have occurred or may not have been heard by everyone.

You need to assess your personal safety. Consider your best option.

This may include staying in a classroom behind a locked door, hiding or self evacuating.

Self Evacuation, which means exiting the school and leaving the campus, is an option.

If you're in a hallway, a common area or near an exterior door, Self Evacuation may be your best choice.

Once you've arrived at a safe location, you should immediately check in with your parents and the school district to let them know you are safe.

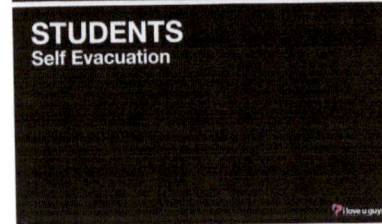

Voice Over:

When law enforcement begins the evacuation, here is what to expect: An officer will unlock your door and enter the room. Stay where you are. An officer will give you specific instructions you must follow.

"It's Broomfield Police Department. You're safe, everything is OK, we're going to get you out of the building. I need everyone to follow my instructions. I need a single file line, leave all of your personal property on the floor where it is. Form a single file line, right here at the door. Teacher, I need you in front please."

You'll be asked to leave your stuff behind, form a line at the door with the teacher in front... "I need everyone to hold hands with the person to the right and left." Hold hands with the person in front of and behind you until you reach your final destination. Wait quietly for further instructions from the officer.

"Teacher, I need you to walk out and follow the instructions of that officer right there. Go ahead." You will be told to proceed to the next officer. Walk, do not run and do not talk. "Walk towards the stairs."

Follow the directions of the officers guiding you during the evacuation. They could be giving you verbal directions or hand signals. Watch the pace of your line. Be aware of obstacles, such as corners, fallen objects, debris or stairs, which may affect the speed your line can move.

Don't stop till you reach the location you were directed to.

"Keep moving. All the way to the end of the fence."

Verify attendance and wait for further instructions.

POLICE
Evacuation is a little different

POLICE
Evacuation is a little different

STUDENT
Instructions

STUDENTS
Keep your hands empty and visible

When capable, it's important to keep your hands visible to the officers.

STUDENTS
Leave your stuff behind

Most likely, you will be asked to leave your stuff behind.

STUDENTS
Bring your phone

If your phone is in your pocket, bring it. If it's in your purse or backpack, you may not be given the opportunity to grab it.

STUDENTS
Don't be surprised if they are loud

Don't be surprised if the officers are loud and demanding. They don't know the extent of the incident yet. They will give direct instructions that you should follow. Again be sure to keep your hands visible.

TEACHER
Instructions

All of that goes for teachers as well. There may be circumstances where you can't bring your purse, briefcase or backpack. Try to bring your keys and wallet.

TEACHERS Grab attendance sheet	Also, grab the attendance sheet.
TEACHERS Bring your phone	And your phone.
TEACHERS At evacuation area, take attendance	At the evacuation assembly area take attendance. If you were able to take attendance during Lockdown, verify students in the assembly area against the roster you created during Lockdown. If everything is OK, show the green card.
DISCUSSION: Do you have permission to self evacuate?	Do you have permission to self evacuate? Yes. Pay attention to the situation. Do you know where the threat is? Can you see the exit? Is it away from the threat, noise or commotion? Remember though, a locked door is proven time barrier. Staff, same answer. But don't leave the students.
DISCUSSION: If you do self evacuate, where do you go?	If you do self evacuate, where do you go? Another school or nearby business Recreational center A friend's house Your house or a family member's house. Be sure to let your parents and the school know.
DISCUSSION: Knock, Knock. Police! Open up.	Knock, Knock. Police! Open up. In a Lockdown, prior to a police led evacuation, don't open the door for anyone. Police or administration will unlock the door.
DISCUSSION: What can you take with you?	What can you take with you? It's unlikely that you can bring your backpack. You may not even be able to get into it, once police enter the room. But if you can, bring your phone, wallet, and keys.
DISCUSSION: Why do we keep our hands visible?	Why do we keep our hands visible? Law enforcement officers are trained that hands can hold dangerous things. They will want to see your hands. You might be asked to evacuate hand in hand, or with your hands on your head.

What will police do? In some cases, during the evacuation assembly, officers will want to verify that students aren't at further risk. They may search students and staff for other dangerous items.	**DISCUSSION:** What will Police do?
Some of you may have heard the term "Shelter-in-place." If you deep dive the FEMA web site, you'll find over a dozen different things to do for Shelter-in-place. Why not go directly to the Hazard and Safety Strategy.	**SHELTER** For Hazard using Safety Strategy
So, what's a hazard? Something dangerous. It could be environmental, like a tornado or earthquake. It might be something like a chemical spill nearby.	**HAZARD?** A danger or risk.
Your safety strategy is what you do in response to the hazard. Public address might be just the hazard and safety strategy. Or it could be "Shelter for the stated hazard using the stated safety strategy." In either case we repeat it.	**STRATEGY** The action or plan to remain safe.
For example. "Tornado, get to the storm shelter. Tornado, get to the storm shelter." **DIY: Please localize these conversations to safety strategies for your hazards.** **Verify this direction with local emergency planner.**	**TORNADO** ...t to the storm shelter
In earthquake country, the safety strategy is drop, cover, and hold.	**EARTHQUAKE** Drop cover and hold
For a hazmat risk, we would seal the room by taping plastic around doors, vents, and windows.	**HAZMAT** Seal vents and doors
In coastal areas, tsunamis are a possibility after an earthquake. Going to high ground or further inland is that hazard's safety strategy.	**TSUNAMI** Get to high ground

DURING SHELTER Always listen for instructions	Listen for instructions. The situation may be very dynamic.
DURING SHELTER Be prepared for the unexpected	Always be prepared for the unexpected.
TEACHERS If possible, take attendance	During a shelter event, teachers should try to take attendance and note the time.
SRP-2025 Standard Response Protocol HOLD SECURE LOCKDOWN EVACUATE SHELTER	Those are all five actions in the Standard Response Protocol
HANDOUTS Share with parents	Please go home and share what you learned with your parents. The "I Love U Guys" Foundation has parent handouts on the website.
Adams 12 Five Star Schools	This presentation would not be possible without the materials originated by Adams 12, Five Star Schools and the City and County of Broomfield Police and Emergency Manager's office.
PEACE. It does not mean to be in a place where there is no noise, trouble, or hard work. It means to be in the midst of those things and still be calm in your heart.	Peace. It does not mean to be in a place where there is no noise, trouble, or hard work. It means to be in the midst of those things and still be calm in your heart.
i love u guys FOUNDATION	

www.ingramcontent.com/pod-product-compliance
Lightning Source LLC
Chambersburg PA
CBHW081549040426

42448CB00015B/3270